RAINS RAIN

Matthew Roth

FUTURECYCLE PRESS

www.futurecycle.org

Cover artwork, NightCafe AI ("flooding from too much rain, washing away, swirling waters, muted watercolor style, brush strokes visible"), interior and cover design by Diane Kistner; Adobe Garamond Pro text and Ocean Sans titling

Library of Congress Control Number: 2022951032

Published by FutureCycle Press
Athens, Georgia, USA

ISBN 978-1-952593-49-9

For Kerry, Ella, and Silas

Contents

ONE

TWO

THREE

Notes
Acknowledgments

ONE

Way and Wood

Too often I find myself
a noun without a verb
to take me for a gambol
down the path to anywhere,
or else I'm all urge and no substance,
a verb, unsponsored and unbound,
vain wind in a lunar landscape
where no tree stands.
On those days, Lord,
when it seems too much to be
two things at once, find me
one word to be and do,
a way and a wood
where the meaning is plain, where
flowers flower, falls fall, rains rain.

The Peach Tree

Because my daughter came home in tears
from the birthday party and could not be
consoled, I have taken her out to harvest
what's left of the garden, whose splendor

has begun to run to rot and squalor
in the haze of August heat. Still,
the beanpoles stand bound and heavy
with knotted vines and here and there

a ripe tomato hangs ready for her hand
to grasp it, twist, and pull it free.
Why can't I bear to ask her
what it was some other innocent

did or said, or didn't do or didn't say?
Instead, I try to keep her close and hope
our work together will be enough to make
the sting subside. But when I turn to look

for her she's gone, running from me
towards the young peach, halfway up
the slope, where we planted it three years ago.
All summer we've watched amazed

the swelling fruit beneath whose weight
the slender branches bend, drooping at their ends.
Though they've turned to butter and crimson,
the peaches aren't yet ripe, and I tell her

not to pick them but she pays no mind,
then yelps and comes to show me how
one side of the peach she holds in her hand
crawls with bugs who have eaten away

half the flesh, revealing the stone at its middle.
If we're going to save them, we'll have to
harvest now, before they are ready,
let them ripen the rest of the way inside.

We'll have to lay them out on the table
by the window where, when she's finally off
to bed, I'll stand in the settling dark,
watching the evening rake its black loam

over the lawn and the garden going
to seed and then the solitary tree,
its free, unburdened branches bowed
as if still beneath that weight.

Inheritance

From the window this morning I watch
my father, snowy-headed and stooped,

go out, dragging a length of logging chain
behind him, to his orchard.

With the chain I know he will beat the trunks
of the four recalcitrant apple trees who refuse,

though old enough, he says, to flower
as they should—a trick his father came to

one hot summer when
by accident he scarred the bark

of an apple tree, only to see
white blossoms burst in mid-July.

"Some of them will only produce
if they think they're going to die."

My son, not seven, joins me at the window,
and seeing what I've seen, he asks me to explain.

Before the first dark line of trees
my father slows, as if forgetting why he came,

then disappears into the mottled shade.
The silence fills us up to overflow.

There is knowledge I could pass to him.
I tell him I don't know.

The Quiet One

To be not small but merely here,
as a letter lost in a long word
larded with odd alliances,
where words hide all their silences.
To be the M in Mnemosyne, seen
but not heard, like a rich man's ward,
or the fat forgotten wife
of a long-remembered bard.
Better yet to be the silent e
that makes the small i speak its name.
That was my way until one day
a child, looking half like me, traced my form
with his finger, a child's game,
and guiltless, smiling, spoke my name.

Debris

The boy says, Dad did you know there are half a million pieces
of space junk orbiting the earth?

We are sitting at the kitchen table.

Then he says, those are just the ones bigger than a marble.

We are sitting together there because his sister has friends over
and his mother is teaching music lessons in the living room.

I say, I am trying to read this. I say, I need to concentrate.

The junk is left over from other missions, he says.

I ask, have you done your homework yet?

Some pieces move 17,000 miles per hour.

Have you cleaned your room?

And that half million is just the pieces large enough to be tracked.

I know you haven't practiced your cello.
I know you haven't taken out the trash.

He says, there's at least a million more pieces of debris
too small for the instruments to see.

Then I look at the boy and say,
I wish for once you would listen to me
and do what you're supposed to do.

I say, I wish you were more like your sister.

Even tiny flecks of paint decades old are dangerous, he says,
because you can't see them coming
and they move so fast.

Fatherly Gesture

In the damp, untutored grass of our summer yard
I tell my son to retreat a little more—
two steps, now another two—and float the hard
magenta disc his way. But my aim is poor
and he takes off like an eager labrador,
trying to track it, though he lacks the speed
and intuition he needs to gauge how far
afield his father's failed attempts will lead.
When I manage at last a level try
he raises his hand too late. The frisbee hits
him hard on his brow. He's stunned, then starts to cry,
then runs inside to show his mom what hurts,
leaving me there in the backyard, statuesque—
frozen in place, still with my arm outstretched.

Silence

Too soon an engine chuffs me awake
to watch as morning trawls its grappling hook
through the silted dark till it catches
and aches to winch blunt forms—
ridges, rooflines, and closer,
the coop and ragged hedgerow—
each of them dragged to the surface
of the day like a battered bus
drawn up from a quarry's flooded floor.

At Echo Lake, remember, the children cried,
welcoming back with wonder
their prodigal voices. Though I try
I can't hear them. I can only recall
the idea of certain sounds—
the feral bliss of porcupines
mating beneath our bedroom window,
or the tight wire of your whisper
when we couldn't be alone.

Through the double pane, daylight deposits
a bed of lilies beside the lawn,
then the whole house goes off
at once, all the rooms alarmed
by the overnight news, the traffic
and weather, and the children
rise, woozy and swooning,
then little by little, room by room,
gain speed, gain speed, until
the roar outside draws them running
and roars them away.

Behind them, silence heals over us
like the skin of a lake
whose silence is not peace,
whose silence is listening.

Without Us

On the television I watch
The World Without Us growing up
in our absence to kudzu and witchgrass
or crumbling away, everything we loved most,

lost. My own house, in common speech,
is a pig sty, a bomb site, a full-blown
disaster of my own making, yet leave
it unoccupied, though the floors

for once are soundly swept,
the table set, the beds in all quarters
untumbled and hospital-cornered—
leave it alone and it goes to pieces,

its immune system weakened
by the simplest of diseases:
mere absence, the thought
of which might even please us

as a man with a family might
decide, for no reason that he can admit,
to take a sabbatical from his own life,
from his living in it, from all the small

heartaches and pleasures that plague us,
retiring instead to his own mental Vegas.
And though he's gone missing only
in spirit, when he tries to come back

he finds nothing left, the old house gone,
the one he tried to forget,
and the new house isn't ready yet.
On my television, the Brooklyn Bridge

untethers itself from Brooklyn, from Bridge.
What we thought was finished needs always
to be restored or repainted, revised and amended,
like an ill-conceived nation, or the bridge

will be ruined by simple oxidization.
Just the air sitting there
like a brown moth on a brown bell
exerts more pressure than we can tell.

Even this poem, uninhabited, won't survive
without you, reader, scuffing the floors,
raiding the fridge, losing change
in the gape of an odd caesura. Shakespeare knew:

So long as eyes can see…so long lives this…
Now the Crystal Cathedral lists, heaves left,
and caves. Now the White House falls.
As the ants celebrate their inauguration

I confess to a kind of grim fascination.
See how they graph the white marble
with perfect black rows
stretching out to the margins like prose.

Randkluft

Beware when traversing
from glacier to granite
the *randkluft,* a nasty crevasse
the Germans invented
to teach us loss.
Though ice and snow
need a rockface to rest on,
proximity can barely mean
without some dead space
in between. It's natural proof
that the world's relations
always stand a bit aloof.
Even a mother,
her sleeping child
curled on her lap,
might confess she feels it—
the creeping recession,
and then, the gap.

On Prayer

These days I want so badly to pray,
but how when I pray so badly, when words
spoil the moment they bud on my tongue,
sour fruit I'd be worse than Cain to offer.

Yet I am taught that God prefers
this aimless proffer to my silence,
which, I admit, too often proves
less meditative than aloof.

So instead and again I turn to the creeds,
which may seem bland but at least are vetted.
Better these than my own prayers
be heard, and answered, and regretted.

Devil's Lake

We thought why not let the map decide
so pointed to nothing and knew
some road must go there.
Across washouts patched with deadfall
and river rock our little car crept
until the lake opened its eye,
silver slash in the umbral sprucewood.
Someone, on a tree, had carved *Lac du Diable*.
Someone, on a day, had imagined us,
the hiss of our boat slicing through
the bright water as we made
for the high unnamable cliffs
that rose from the other shore.

Stars

Still primitive, nosing the glade, making
tracks in the trackless, riparian rough,
mere mammals sussing the underbrush,
suspirious, inconsiderate of desire
or disaster, we starred the gulch
of moist maidenhair, impressed
them as we bedded down
in a brown wool blanket where
we twined, we mated, sure,
like porcupines beneath a porch
of midnight sky, siderealized and vulgar
as all mythic lovers, and I,
drunk on the dew of you,
brackened and salt-starved, swore
to myself, my first betrayal,
I'd never elegize the lithe,
unpunctuated arc of those first hours,
would not dissect with whetted words
our frowsy, fernlicked bodies, fused
in a moment's outcry, though I knew,
even then I knew I lied, and just
outside the light of our fire already
I could hear the sibilant shiver,
the hushed, anticipatory hum,
of what we have, at last, become.

The News

When the news comes for you, as it's bound to come,
you will know you've been swimming for years
toward the surface of this day, this day

when the news fills you up like a lung, like air
surprising the diver, who, having lived too long
in that slow, dreamlike buoyancy of the sea,

forgets how substanceless, griefless
the air can be, all that sunlight smashing
the black water to pieces. Some of you

will leave the sea behind, climb willingly
into the possible, feeling your legs,
shaking them out, first one and then the other,

and some of you will turn, return to the sea,
diving deeper this time, down past the reef
with its travesty of companionship,

deeper to where there is no light but the light
of dark swimmers, finning by without fear
or expectation, impossibly lit from within.

TWO

Innogen

A "ghost character" from Shakespeare's *Much Ado about Nothing*, she enters at the beginning of the play but does not speak and never appears again. Most scholars consider her presence a mistake, a leftover character from an early draft.

I do not know who made me, but I was made.
I had a name, a role (*his wife*), and I
with the rest made my entrance, courteously,
onto that stage, that world, where our drama played.
Did I speak? I did not. The others seemed
to have a better sense than I how best
to spur the action on, how to impress
the ear with words my mute mind never dreamed.
Could I have known that entrance, that brief scene,
would be my last, and yes, my only chance
to make my mark (and still I know not how)—
could I have known I'd live a ghost, unseen,
untouched by love or fate or happenstance,
might I have spoken then? Enough. I'm done
with you, whoever you are, and what
your forms allow. I'm speaking now.

Lilacs

Their sensuality
uncouples
the causal chain,
cold reason's power,
as if the scent itself
burst into flower,
as thoughts might
compose a brain
or love the heart,
life imitating art.

Anchor

In the old old story, a splintering crash
drew the congregants out from their Sabbath prayers
to find a ship's anchor lodged in the ground,
one scarred iron fluke hooked in the doorframe
of the church and a tether leading up
to the unmistakable hull of a ship
floating in the air above the steeple.

Some gasped and some fell to their knees
when a man who looked like them appeared,
a man who leapt from the side of the ship
and swam down through the air as if in water,
as if holding his breath, and tried to free
the anchor but could not. Some of the men
moved to grab him then but the bishop said

no, let him go, for he will surely drown,
so they watched as the man drew a knife
from between his teeth and cut the rope,
swam back to the ship, and pulled himself
aboard as it began to sail away, its sails
moved by the very wind that moved the trees
and ruffled the bishop's long black robe.

At last the ship disappeared from sight and only
the anchor remained, its new testament first
a sign of wonder, then of patience, then,
when all were long dead, a sign of what remains
of what was once a metaphor for what,
if ever it came, is never coming back again.

And now the anchor too is lost, though scholars
have marked the most likely site. Here a replica stands
by a gift shop church where all are invited to pay
for keychains and chocolate miniatures
of the anchor and the ship that sailed away.

Now Everything

is alien and soft as the suited corpse,
the rote grace of the hour
ceremonial and bland. You stand,
dark and polished as an unbitten plum,
in the palm of the afternoon,
whose practiced gestures offer
no relief or revelation, nothing
to be reopened or unsealed.
The distracted sun, for its part, declines
to blind you. Only the rain, seeping
from the poplar shade, in good faith
cools the body, speaking for no one.
When it's over, the last sound
is the sound of slowness passing,
of something dragging its silver trail
across the damp stones of your attention.

Primer

The gun is certified to teach
me justice. Ardent company.
What else would you christen it,
the bullet? This oblivious clot
of twisted elm teaches me
to face the wind flagless
before an empty plain.
This bowl of rain
imagines a circle of sky
but not my face, interposed, suspicious.
Lord, it is true, I have prayed
without ceasing. Yet what do I make
but a map of failure? Even that
so soon obsolete. I must not be
too precious. For the last time
I instruct my children to go outside.
They laugh and go outside.
Every lesson is not a prayer,
mister. But what else
would you call it? The wind
collects dust and the wind
lets it fall in swirls and skeins
on the empty plain.
Somewhere west of here
an ocean is teaching me
patience, how to offer no relief,
incunabula of nothing but clouds.

The Cause

This man is the enemy, they said. Will you shoot him?
I said, I could never shoot anyone.

But you wouldn't have to look at him, they said,
you could do it from the sky. Just push this button.

I refused.

But he's hardly a man at all, they said.
Really he's a monster.
Really he's a roach.

I don't believe that, I said.
I will not kill him.

But what will you do, they asked, to support the cause?

I said, come with me, and I took them into the garden,
its beds spilling over with vegetables and flowers.
Some of the flowers were the color of sky,
some the color of fire.

This is what I have done instead, I said,
holding out a red tomato in each hand.

And this is what we did for you, one of them said,
and he showed me a picture of the man
lying dead on the ground.

The Sentence

From the pure fog, from the milk of silence,
you have come, sensibly dressed for the journey,
as the train lurches out from the station
even before you find your seat, the train
whose route spans in a breath the gap
between Arcturus and Albany, where a detour
sends you meandering through barrens of sand
and pine, now slowing to climb the bright spike
of a lupine flower, spiraling up the green stem
and purple raceme till you reach the top,
rolling to a stop where the bloom meets the sky
and the station master, a blue butterfly,
unspools before you in the mid-day sun
the precise evolution of his tongue.

Excess

is like the lilac hedge
whose beauty you couldn't bear
to prune for fear of losing
even a season's blooms.
Then you're standing
in the lightless living room
bemoaning the twiggy lattice
grown up like briars around
an enchanted palace.
The experts say you can't
just hack them back. It's wise
to go lightly, in stages, though
it may take a few unsightly ages
to get everything back to proper size.
With luck new growth will sprout.
Or (and why not) buy a big truck
and yank them out.

Hollow

Matter should grow denser
towards its center,

but it's not that consistent,
so the wall where your fist went

turned out, thank God, to be hollow
as the fine, almost weightless, bones of a sparrow

flying through the great hall
of an old metaphor (you'll recall)

where life is the air and the light and the room
that opens, a bloom

in the night's dark garden, a gap
in the unremitting black

we thought so solid it could not open
a space to hope in.

Man and Crumb: Ars Poetica

Look here,
a man,
and here,
on the countertop,
a crumb.

The clock,
struck dumb
between chimes,
offers ordinary time,
nothing more
to deliver.

Look hard enough
and you may detect
in each figure
the slightest shiver.

Sonnet Nabokov: Hummingbird Moths

Near the end of June all the colors collapsed
At once, the lilac's purple bleeding to gray
Beneath a moist, young moon. A low buzz passed
Overhead, a streak in the dying light of day.
Keen with desire, I followed that telltale song.
Olive and pink, it hovered in the bower,
Vibrating its halo, and dipped its long tongue,
Volute and voluptuous, into a flower.
Or later, in autumn, when there came a freeze,
Killing my mother's flowers all at once,
One could sugar for moths by painting the trees
Black with molasses, slathered across their trunks.
Ablaze in the light of my lantern, they would feed,
Not knowing how their hunger fed my need.

Against Machines

Had I not found myself in need of connection
to all the light and heat and motion they give
in return, and at great cost, for my affection—
machines in my pockets, machines I drive,

or stolid, grave reactors, flashing their lights
to warn at night the careless pilot who
flies too close to the ground, unaware what heights
our vigilant machines are rising to—

then I would not this hour imagine my death
as meltdown, as nosedive, as a powering off
of sight and sound, of tongue and heart and breath.
Rather, I'd see a leaf decaying, soft

beneath the branches of a maple tree,
or a slip of sand dissolving, grain by grain,
diminished without force or urgency
in this cool, uncalculating summer rain.

Duration

Resonant bowl, struck horizon's humming.
Snuffed by the howl of anonymous freight.
Or your mother's voice, eaten

by the bleating of lambs. Each moment
constricts, an eye dispersing the useful miniatures
of mind for its own bright feather, still miles

from the feather's bright bird.
Your mother will not keep inside
the ovine chorus, thinning like vapor into air.

In a desert, water falls inside us,
persisting not by will but form,
endemic irrigation that binds and carries.

So your mother has eaten her voice
into you. Even now it returns, ravenous
for context, without portent, boon, or harm.

On Memory

Take the grave rubbers
collecting with a sigh
the wind-worn lovers
laid beside the babe
with matching fate.
Take the ancient crocodile,
Sappho-stuffed, without
an expiration date.
Take Lenin stewing in a bottle.
Take Mao beneath the sheen of glass.
Give me instead some winter snow
the freezer kept, surprising
June's green grass.

Ephemera

Like a fumbling after words,
the cloud's dark middle,
anything the air holds
broken and willing.

The word survives nothing
beyond the mouth of its maker—
so warm breath on the neck,
on the windowpane.

And yet, I have seen
frail fingers of steam
rise up from the mouth
of an empty cup.

Resurrection

If you want
that sweetness
on your tongue
drizzled with honey
ricotta-stuffed
or falling apart
in jam jars
row on row
you will dig
this grave
scar the
green yard
in the middle
of autumn
and with your
sharp spade
violently slice
the roots
in a circle
halfway round
and lay
the fig tree
down to
be buried
throughout
the long season
until come spring
you dig it out
and set it right
and pray
to whatever
makes the fig
forgive you

and give you again
what you say
you want
that sweetness
and then
the amen.

Tether

The eye is a mouth to ruin, a throat
the bruised world passes through,
softer as it goes. Soon, the station

lights blink out, walls fall
away to some humdrum dream
of what a wall might be. I'm left,

my ear chained to a chain-
choked dog, far off, who knows
no end of care. I want to want

the air like that, to strike the first surprise
a sudden turning sends my way:
a rock, a cloud, the quaking tamarack

out back my sisters tied me to one fall.
I tried for hours to wish them back,
though later they cried and kissed me till

I wished them all away. Faces fade.
Each square of window glass recites
its long division of the air.

Only the stars are hard tonight,
too bright each blade the darkness carves
and sharpens to a point.

THREE

On Miracles

I decided to take myself for a walk in the country because I was feeling a little put off by the bustle and vanity of the world, a nice phrase I think I picked up from James Makepeace Thackeray. Oh, but everything here was pretty mundane, too. Sand on the roadside. Chicory flowers. One ant fighting another slightly bigger ant. Even Mary Oliver, I feel certain, would have been a little bored. Then out of the unmown grass a box turtle, not quite suddenly, advanced, wearing a tiny sky-blue t-shirt with holes for all four legs. The turtle paused, looking straight ahead at something in the road or on the other side of the road. Hey little fella, I said, stooping down to pick it up so I could examine its shirt. On the belly side was printed the following: PLEASE TURN ME OVER. Oh, I see, I said aloud. Do you? said the turtle. Holy wow! is not a phrase I admire, but that is what I said in reply. The turtle, for its part, proceeded then to relate how it got the shirt (overly helpful farm girl), also some of its dietary restrictions (no shellfish), a dream it had last night where the craziest thing happened (extra leg), and its unfortunate route (via dolorosa) across the meadow that morning. At which point I was so bored that I set the turtle down and continued walking to where I had parked my car, then drove back to the city more convinced than ever that country life was not for me.

Extremities

Today everything is either the best or the worst, the greatest or the least. The grass in the median strip? Nothing ever so green. The ant dragging a dead beetle through the dust? The most industrious ant and also, I am certain, the strongest. I could not be more disappointed, however, in these irises, whose flowers emerged dishwater yellow, my least favorite color. And this coffee coating my World's Greatest Poet mug? The absolute dregs. I must tell you I would count myself the unluckiest person in the world were it not for my friends, the best friends I could have. Tom here, for instance, has written the year's funniest novel, or else the saddest, and you should read it. My friend Morrey was a scholar of Methodism but now he is buying a sawmill, the best solution to middle age I can think of. Though if, as sometimes happens to sawyers, he cuts off his hand on the toothy blade, it might be the worst solution. Take infinite care, Morrey! My own hands are so weak they flap in the wind, which, to be fair, approaches hurricane force. Something is going to happen, and then something else. It's going to be amazing, one way or another. Already for the beetle, things have gone about as bad as they could go. Imagine walking through the world like this. How straight the furrow in the farmer's field, how distant the universe and a single stalk of corn, barely visible in the twilight, which lingers so long it must be some kind of record.

The Peace of Wild Things

When I despair that LeninPutinXX and his tricked-out M3 ThunderWasp tank with unlimited power-ups has again purposely and without provocation singled out my tank for destruction even though I am no danger to him, I close my laptop and go for a little jaunt on the path behind my house to where it ends at a small, pleasant stream called Trout Run. There I spy my neighbor's three male ducks trying like everything to have sex with his one female duck, whose vagina, I have recently learned, has multiple blind alleys into which she can direct the sperm of the dullard rapists whose genetic line she wants no part of. Eventually one of them grabs her neck in his bill and forces her head underwater and mounts her while the others skulk off until it's their turn, and I go and walk a few yards downstream only to scare a croaking blue heron up out of the cattails where he was no doubt standing perfectly motionless, as he has stood pretty much every day of his life, hoping an unlucky frog or small fish will swim by so he can strike clean through its body with his giant death spear, swallow it whole, then go right back to work. The gnats are terrible this year, so I go back inside, glancing once at the stack of unfinished work on my desk, then log into one of those lower-tier battles full of light-armor noobs I can totally dominate, and am free.

Induction

At the English Department Honors Society gathering I read the inductees a small poem of encouragement and admiration before we pass out the shredded pages and ritual vat of blood. When they have covered themselves entirely there are always one or two who take it too far, having papered over their mouths and noses so thoroughly they find it hard to breathe. The problem is their panicked eyes, absent the rest of their panicked facial features, appear no different than the eyes of their peers, an odd fact I am saving for later use.

Bigfoot

That Sunday I went to church but I couldn't go in. All the words had become strange to me. Attend, attendant, tights, bent knee, satin pillow bearing a child's gold spoon. I couldn't go in so I set off down the lane, past the cemetery, the parishioners, our parish of root, our parish of soil. Just needed to clear my head. It wasn't long before I saw him coming up the road, a kind of long bouncy stride, a pep in his step, my mother would have said. Bigfoot, I called, to no response. I'm sorry—Sasquatch. Old habits! Bigfoot stopped and looked me over, pursing his lips and squinching them to the side in a gesture I recognized as skepticism. He was carrying a paper sack, rolled down at the top. What's in the bag, I asked, just to make conversation. I was feeling unprepared. Already I was aware that later, when Bigfoot was gone, I would foster regrets. Carefully Bigfoot opened the sack and reached in with his hairy fingers. Plum, he said, offering me one. It was suspiciously cold. This is a metaphor, isn't it. You're a metaphor, I said, or an allusion, a literary allusion, or religious. I know, you're Jesus! Why does everything have to be about something else, Bigfoot said, kind of annoyed, in the voice of my dead mother.

On Doctrine

At first it's satisfying, how good
the hammer feels in the hand
as the soft wood yields to the glamorous
bite of the galvanized nail. Even
mistakes prove opportune chances
to review technique, and soon
smooth board abuts smooth board,
though your knees are sore
and your left thumb throbs
from an errant blow. Who will blame you
when, near the end of your task,
the last hot nail grotesquely bends,
like you, at the waist. And though
you know you should pry it free,
the box of nails is out of reach
and the sun, all day attacking
your back, won't dim.
Screw that. Just swing the hammer
and pound that sucker flat.

Quicksand

"To survive, the victim needs simply
to lie on his back."

It's nice for a while, of course,
as if the world tipped forward
ninety degrees and all you can see
are the leaves
painting a pale, waxing moon,
as you lie there, swooning,
a spoon afloat
a bowl of boiled oats.
But soon, mere survival,
as instinct, succumbs
to more distinct rivals—
that burger, that blonde—
equally vital to your kind's evolution:
survival is fine, but it's not a solution.

Ingenious Machine

On the eighth day
of rain I drove back
to the city. In the mall
the commons brimmed
with precision and the red-
haired girl at Hong's Wok
wore a ring on a chain
around her neck.
When she leaned
forward to count
my change it swung
between us, a pendulum
making time inside
our brief incorruptible clock.

The Argument

When at last it is over
the storm collects itself

in small, irregular depressions
he steps around on his way

to work. Made to linger
at a crosswalk, he is tempted

to see in each reflection
some promise

of another heaven,
another sky.

Of course
they are really

quite shallow,
and tomorrow, dry.

Regret

Crossing the river-
colored light

simple and brown
as the soul must be

all eyes and the roots
drop off

strange current I kept
thinking go back

Bridge

We were crossing the black river
when the jaws of some old figure
or forgotten rhetoric cracked open
like a drawbridge beneath us.
The shores that afternoon were lined
with concrete shops selling frozen yogurt
and taco bowls. Beyond them summer
rippled the reef of the cityscape.
Helicopters and small planes circled
the sun. We are running out of air,
you said, but it's not important.
A little man in a uniform hopped and waved,
then a siren, or some kind of alarm,
drowned out your voice. Still
we were crossing the black river.
If that really is a river, I thought
but did not say, if that's the river,
darling, why doesn't it move?

Loser

In the Museum of Lost Time, displays are replete
with special finds of every kind. See here,
the duck-billed hippo, whose four syndactyl feet
paddled the ancient, Nilotic deeps, or veer
into the flightless wing, where you'll meet a kind
of proto-emu with variegated bones
who once called proto-Indiana home.
He's a wonder, to be sure, of chance or design,
yet he might have been, in his own dark eon,
wholly unimpressive, too bland to woo
a mate, his brain so muddled he chose, in lieu
of a puddle, a pit of tar in which to clean
himself. A dullard, he's now the star of our pageant,
our kinship warmer than we like to imagine.

The New Math

When they tell us about the new math
we feel foolish, old math being all we knew,
and true to us as far as we knew it.
Whole blackboards hence grow gray
with erasure, making way for what
the new math has to say. Yet no matter
how hard we scrub or cleanly we chalk
the new proofs, a stubborn haze,
a ghostly residue, of the old math
bleeds through. So it was with her,
and with me, and with you.

Relative Weight

The Blue Whale's heart, they say, is heavy
as the car I drove to work today.

And just as relevant,
its tremendous tongue is equal to

one full-grown elephant.
It's true, we like to know

what equals what,
if only because it's fun

to balance an elephant and a tongue
on the mind's teeter-totter.

I dissent. Such fodder
misleads, at best.

What happens when the whale
grows greater, or the elephant less?

And I should note that to the whale,
one tongue is badly spent

when exchanged for an elephant,
no matter the size or scale

of its development. Still honesty
requires me to confess my own

abuse of gravity, how just
this morning I cursed

in earnest my lost house key,
while half a world away they gathered

the nameless dead from a vast tsunami.
Somehow their thousands appeared

to me almost bereft of weight,
so light their bodies could be

outweighed by the heft
of that single, absent key.

For Brodsky

A modest little country by the sea,
a half-blind street, and once inside
we sit for supper and you say
all you can tell for certain is the time.

The sun always sets behind the TV tower.
Dearest, what's the point
of light, heat, cold, or darkness,
of the gray, dank city that freezes bare.

I am speaking to you and it's not my fault
I am already half an invalid,
like a church lost somewhere amid the fields.
I guess it's one's soul that makes one pray.

Once you know the future, you can make it come
and dwindle into a little star.
Life without us is, darling, thinkable.
How far all this is from prayer.

Aftermath

When at last you swore yourself free
you came and walked the hour with me
until we found a field of hay
and waded in waist-high, then lay
together there beneath the blue
permissive sky. It all felt new—
soft grass, soft bodies, kissing you—
and no one ever found us.

But soon the weight of lying there
became too much. I pulled your hair
by accident and the sharp jab
of spring's first cutting scratched and stabbed
us through our clothes. You turned your wrath
on the ants that crawled beneath the grass,
and all this time the aftermath
was growing up around us.

Leaving the Hospital

Nothing that rises is lost
even gray mist ghosting
the steeples the whitewashed
careless steeples
you said you wanted
to disappear
like a ship in heavy seas
or flung like blind arrows
in battle by the tracks
we felt the vibration
worms tunneled
beneath our feet
like the worst kind
of secrets you put your ear to
the ground you said
quiet you said
listen

Origami

Fashion a sheet
of proper shape
for what you want
to make. Now slowly
sweep your palm
across its flat
expanse and hear
in the sky
above that wave
washing the sand
a laughing gull's
harsh cry.

Why

Because the land has balled its fingers into fists,
    bruised hard with winter light.

Because the pond behind my house has closed
    its silver eye, sealed for sleep.

Because familiar shibboleths—Pemigewasset
    and Monadnock—glide easily off my tongue.

Because Winnipesaukee has swallowed another
    machine, its headlights fishing back at us.

Because the snow is falling faster and will stay.

Because I'm awake to see.

Because the mountain I live on looms beyond sight.

Because a fire paints the sky with trees.

Because snow falls darkly beyond this burning.

Because fire burns hotter in light of this snow.

Because I love the one who made this fire tonight.

Because love is the business of fire, the heat
    and the light.

Notes

"For Brodsky": In this cento, all of the language in the poem is culled from the poetry of Joseph Brodsky.

"On Memory": Many fragments of the Greek poet Sappho's writing were found on papyri used to stuff the insides of mummified crocodiles in ancient Egypt.

"The Peace of Wild Things" is a send-up of Wendell Berry's famous poem of the same name.

"Sonnet Nabokov: Hummingbird Moths" draws on language and imagery from a paragraph in chapter six of Vladimir Nabokov's memoir, *Speak, Memory.*

Acknowledgments

14 Magazine: "Devil's Lake"
32 Poems: "Extremities," "The Quiet One," "Quicksand"
Bennington Review: "Bigfoot"
Birmingham Poetry Review: "Stars," "The Peace of Wild Things"
Delmarva Review: "Debris," "Fatherly Advice"
Harpur Palate: "Now Everything"
Iron Horse Literary Review: "Randkluft"
Mount Hope Magazine: "Man and Crumb: Ars Poetica," "Tether"
The Northern Virginia Review: "Innogen," "Against Machines"
Potato Eyes: "Why" (as "Why: A New Hampshire Reverie")
Rappahannock Review: "The Peach Tree"
Roanoke Review: "The News"
Rock and Sling: "Resurrection" (as "Resurrection Day")
Ruminate: "Inheritance" (as "My Father Goes Out with a Chain
    in His Hand")
Think: "Relative Weight," "Sonnet Nabokov: Hummingbird Moths"
Third Wednesday: "Hollow," "The Sentence"
The Windhover: "On Doctrine," "On Miracles"

"Anchor" appeared in *This Present Former Glory: An Anthology of Honest Spiritual Literature* (A Game for Good Christians, 2020).

"Innogen" and "Against Machines" received *The Northern Virginia Review*'s 2020 Editors' Prize.

About FutureCycle Press

FutureCycle Press is dedicated to publishing lasting English-language poetry in both print-on-demand and Kindle formats. Founded in 2007 by long-time independent editor/publishers and partners Diane Kistner and Robert S. King, the press was incorporated as a nonprofit in 2012. A number of our editors are distinguished poets and writers in their own right, and we have been actively involved in the small press movement going back to the early seventies.

Each year, we award the FutureCycle Poetry Book Prize and honorarium for the best original full-length volume of poetry we published that year. Introduced in 2013, proceeds from our Good Works projects are donated to charity. Our Selected Poems series highlights contemporary poets with a substantial body of work to their credit; with this series we strive to resurrect work that has had limited distribution and is now out of print.

We are dedicated to giving all of the authors we publish the care their work deserves, offering a catalog of the most diverse and distinguished work possible, and paying forward any earnings to fund more great books. All of our books are kept "alive" and available unless and until an author requests a title be taken out of print.

We've learned a few things about independent publishing over the years. We've also evolved a unique and resilient publishing model that allows us to focus mainly on vetting and preserving for posterity poetry collections of exceptional quality without becoming overwhelmed with bookkeeping and mailing, fundraising activities, or taxing editorial and production "bubbles." To find out more about what we are doing, come see us at futurecycle.org.

The FutureCycle Poetry Book Prize

All original, full-length poetry books published by FutureCycle Press in a given calendar year are considered for the annual FutureCycle Poetry Book Prize. This allows us to consider each submission on its own merits, outside of the context of a traditional contest. Too, the judges see the finished book, which will have benefitted from the beautiful book design and strong editorial gloss we are famous for.

The book ranked the best in judging is announced as the prize-winner in January of the subsequent year. There is no fixed monetary award; instead, the winning poet receives an honorarium of 20% of the total net royalties from all poetry books and chapbooks the press sold online in the year the winning book was published. The winner is also accorded the honor of being on the panel of judges for the next year's competition; all judges receive copies of the contending books to keep for their personal library.

www.ingramcontent.com/pod-product-compliance
Lightning Source LLC
Chambersburg PA
CBHW070010100426
42741CB00012B/3186